SHAKESPEARE'S LADIES

A second book of speeches for women
from the plays of William Shakespeare

EDITED by DICK DOTTERER

Dramaline Publications
36-851 Palm View Road
Rancho Mirage, CA 92270
Phone 619/770-6076 Fax 619/770-4507

Library of Congress Cataloging-in-Publication Data

Shakespeare, William, 1564-1616.
    Shakespeare's ladies : a second book of speeches for
women from Shakespeare's plays / selected, compiled,
and edited by Dick Dotterer.
      p. cm.
    ISBN 0-940669-19-6. (acid-free paper)
    1. Women—Drama. 2. Monologues. I. Dotterer , Dick.
    II. Title.
PR2768.D57   1992
822.3'3—dc20   92-28173

Cover by John Sabel

This book is printed on 55# Glatfelter acid-free paper. A paper that meets the
requirements of the American Standard of Permanence of paper for printed library
material.

CONTENTS

INTRODUCTION

"Speak the speech, I pray you. . . ."

Groan. Gritch. Complain. Moan. And bitch, bitch, bitch.

Okay: So you have an assignment in your acting class shortly that requires a solo piece from a Shakespearean "classic"; or you have an audition soon for a place in a theater company or production, and part of that audition requires at least one piece from a Shakespearean play. But solo speeches are so dense, so complex, such mazes! One always confronts the chance of getting lost in them, and, if that happens, to die! No, no: long, solo passages from Shakespeare and other "classics," usually referred to as "set speeches" (or set pieces), are deathtraps!

There is no denial that set speeches are difficult, and it is a brutal fact of life in the theater that such pieces can be boring (ultimately, the one unforgivable sin in the Theater). Actors have to work harder with a solo than with dialogue. The actor maybe the only one speaking, but an audience does not listen to a complex text unless an actor forces it to do so.

Edith Evans explained her approach to playing Shakespeare this way: you take the last line of the speech and pull it toward you. That statement ranks in all of its simplicity and in all of it complexity with a piece of advice from another eminent actor: "Learn the lines, and don't bump into the furniture." The complexities of those two simple statements lie in how you fulfill the demands of their predicates.

A long speech needs to be discovered line by line and thought by thought as it is spoken. When a player tackles a long speech or set piece it is so easy to fall into the void to play the *summary* of the speech rather than to discover it line by line. Such performances are dull because the player tends to *generalize* the speech rather than pronounce it as if it were being said for the very first time. The actor plays the general mood or emotion that the speech suggests to him/her rather than to dramatize the story the speech tells.

There is another crude fact of life in the theater: an audience's attention wanders if a player does not hold it. Part of the use of these monologues and set pieces is to train the player to hold and to help the audience. In doing the monologue, even more than elsewhere, the actor must be deeply inside the situation of the character. Even the most familiar of set pieces (i. e., "O Romeo, Romeo! Wherefore art thou, Romeo?" "To be or not to be . . .") rise out of the events presented in the text of the play. These monologues do not simply pre-exist as separate arias, plopped down independently of their surrounding countryside. The actor *must find* the language of the speech for himself/herself and make the auditor feel that this speech is being discovered and is being said *for the very first time.*

Too many times the player doesn't look for the story or conflict in the speech—or in the old school of rhetoric parlance, the "argument"—to take the audience on the journey needed. Long speeches, monologues, and soliloquies have a story to tell. It is the actor's job to tell that story. It is the actor's job to take the audience along; to hold the interest of the audience as a storyteller would. Too many times the actor simply issues a "white paper" statement as to the character's static state-of-being at the present moment, and time and the play stand still. An actor has to open himself/herself up to he audience in many of the same ways he/she must open up to other actors in dialogue scenes. The player must *share* his/her need to communicate. The player must make an audience think with him/her as he/she unfolds his/her situation; the audience must feel that the character needs to share his/her problems with it. Theater doesn't happen if the audience sits back at a safe distance (as separated by a sheet of glass) and merely observes the character thinking. The actor *must* make an audience participate; a player must make an audience listen and follow the story-line—the "argument"—of the thought of the speech.

(To digress for a moment, soliloquies need a special note of mention. As with all speeches, soliloquies must rise out of the situation from within the text, it must have a story told, it must be spontaneous, and it must be real; but added to all of that, a soliloquy is a moment in the play of the character's *private* story, as opposed to the character's "public" function. At these private moments the character needs to make the audience feel that he/she is so overwhelmed with the situation at hand that he/she needs to share his/her dilemmas and problems with it.)

Shakespeare's texts demand complete investments of the actor in the words. Shakespeare's playscripts are so rich, so bold, so extraordinary that the player is forced to discover more possibilities in the voice and in emotional delivery than he/she is aware of. The structure of the language and the thought in a Shakespearean text requires both courage and discipline from the actor. The player may *have to become extravagant* because in a very practical way the verbal and physical lives of Shakespeare's characters are symbiotically connected.

There is often a gap between the life the player has going on internally, the energy and imaginative force that is needed to create the reality of the character being portrayed, and the life excitement the player gives the text as he/she speaks it. We are talking about the excitement and the energy a player feels when he/she is working-up the part but that is never felt nor is fully realized when the player commits sparingly to the words of the text. (That is, how the player "reads" to the audience.) This gap between internal creation and external manifestation can be even more apparent in heightened or poetic playscripts where there is *a certain size to the language.* And where the texts have been heard before, which leads to certain expectations by the auditors. Shakespearean texts are inflicted with both. Shakespearean language has a certain size to it, and much of it is familiar to a number of listeners in any given audience. These factors in themselves can be either inhibiting—or exhilarating. (Singers of opera or well-known parts in any lyric theater production must face much the same perplexities when they tackle the challenge to make one of the great arias or well-known songs and/or roles their own.)

Theatrical speech performs several functions all at the same time—still a third hard fact of life in the theater. One of those tasks is to physicalize emotions through words: words are the vehicles for thoughts to become actions. The problem in speaking Shakespeare's verse is two-pronged. First, the actor and the listener must both experience the lines as poetry; and, secondly, the player must make the language sound "natural" to the listener—like a flesh and blood human being putting thoughts and feelings into words, verbalizing his/her intentions and desires as they are happening spontaneously at that given moment.

Dramatic poetry, which the player must make the audience experience, has a combination of two elements in the broadest sense of regards. First is the sense which arises from the context of the line, and the second is the melody of the line, which is derived from the structure of the line or lines. This structure is an organization by which the sense and the implications of that sense are expressed. The melody is the sounds of the words when the player articulates the lines.

A player has to find the right energy for *that* particular text—whatever it might be. The player must find a balance between too interior and controlled energy, in which the delivery of the word is dull, and the too exterior and explosive an energy. In this latter case the words become unfocused and the thought to be expressed simply becomes generalized. Each speech must be treated as a small, well constructed scene. The beginning of the scene, the rising conflict, the climax or turning point, and the denouement leading to the conclusion must be selected, mapped, and journeyed. This can be done only by discovering the specifics of the speech. (This rule of thumb is especially important to practice when the set speech is taken out of its natural context, devoid of it surrounding supports, and is presented to the listener as a dramatic entity on its own.)

Players have a responsibility to the language of the playwright and to his text. Players articulate through the language they bring alive. But speech is more than making the voice sound more interesting. Speech is making language organic. The words spur the sounds, and the flexibility and the range of communication are found because the words of the text require them.

Work on Shakespearean texts opens a player's awareness to language in modern texts and scripts as well. An awareness of language adds resonance to the words a player speaks in contemporary texts, even if those words are cemented in modern "reality" or colloquiality. (And the player who keeps his/her ear attuned to modern colloquiality helps him/her integrate its rhythms and sounds into the speaking of verse.)

Players must always seek balances, for every speech an actor speaks on stage is heightened speech: *It is performed.* And the player must find the particular voice and the placement for that particular language for that particular moment in the text. When the set piece is performed independently, it is even more important that the player bring the language, with its attending senses, emotions, thoughts, and implications, alive and articulated clearly for a precise understanding by the listener.

Players must make what they say remarkable to their audience. This cannot always be done with mediocre scripts and banal dialogue (TV scripts anyone?), but the richer the player's experience is in handling language, the more a competent player can get out of even the most banal of scripts and the most obvious and obtund of dialogue.

THE PURPOSE AND USE OF THIS BOOK

This book contains thirty pieces for actresses culled from twenty-four of Shakespeare's plays. As with other books I have both edited and translated for this series, this book should be thought of as a resource and a tool for the actress in studying the craft and art of acting, Shakespeare, Elizabethan prose, and blank-verse. It should be thought as much a scene-study book as a quick source for Shakespearean audition material. While the selections in this book are on the whole shorter in length than those presented in its two companion volumes, *Shakespeare's Monologues for Women* and *Shakespeare's Monologues They Haven't Heard,* the pieces have been consciously edited and selected so that each of them presents a short scene or an incisive, dramatic moment in the life of the character, a moment on which her emotional dilemma turns. Sometimes, especially with the supporting parts, it is only a moment and a single speech that gives the player the opportunity to illuminate the character. The player must know how to exemplify that moment to its fullest effect. Each selection, then, presents the actress with something to *act.* These pieces have not been chosen merely for pretty poetry. Each piece has a purpose for it being acted.

Moreover, there is much to learn in handling blank-verse, and many of these pieces involve it. Blank verse is something that is not recited in sing-song, nor is it by its very nature "naturalistic" colloquial speech in delivery. Blank verse is a conscious style that requires a technique all of its own to speak. The way it is formed in the speeches gives clues as to how it should be delivered.

There is also a technique to guiding a listener through Shakespearean prose to a clear understanding of the thoughts, emotions, sense, and story that is intended in it. Several selections included in this book were chosen to address this precise problem. Because Shakespeare's texts are so diverse and so dense in their theatrical richness, the selections in this book, or in the companion volumes in this series, can be returned to again and again to address any number of acting problems the player wishes to solve.

The material in this book has been chosen to include the broadest contrasts and types and emotional ranges which Shakespeare addressed in his dramatic writing. The selections are divided into four arbitrary sections: The Histories, the Comedies, the Tragedies, the Romances, and the "Problem" Plays. The pieces are also arranged in order of their composition within the various categories.

Even though this book is designed as a resource, and I have tried to give the actress something from which to build a characterization in each of the individual introductions to the separate selections, it should be self-evident that to do the pieces and the characters justice, the player should make the time to read, even to study, the playscript from which the piece comes. She will then know exactly where the specific piece falls within the dramatic actions' build of the play and its relevancy to the play as a whole.

DICK DOTTERER

PART I: THE HISTORIES

King Henry VI, Part II
QUEEN MARGARET—ACT III, SCENE 2

AGE: Young (Any Age)   Intent: Serious

Margaret of Anjou is married to an imbecilic and weak king in an arrangement made by the man who loves her—a man whose scruples seem to be merely convenient—so that he can be near her; she sees her only son disinherited by his father in favor of her worst enemy and his family; then she experiences the murders of her lover, her son, and her husband; and finally she is thrown down from the heights of power to the ignominity and poverty of a displaced person, harried and crazed by grief and an obsession for revenge. No wonder she is at times unprincipled, vengeful, fierce, audacious, and a virago. She comes to realize she is a woman alone, a woman who must use any means to survive—and to win.

The legendary characteristics of Queen Margaret fascinated Shakespeare. Her dramatic through-line journeys the terrain of four plays, making her character the longest female role in the Shakespearean canon. And, in may ways, Queen Margaret embodies and mirrors the struggle. dissolution, and disintegration of England and its people during the troubled times of "The War of the Roses." She makes her first, brief appearance toward the end of *King Henry VI, Part I*, as a young, beautiful and seemingly overwhelmed girl. She quickly grows to learn the use of the reins of power and the frustration from being thwarted by lesser men with more authority than "a mere woman" who surround her. And, finally, she is the disoriented, emotionally imbalanced ruin of solid stability and strength she once was. This is also the course of English society during the War of the Roses.

In *King Henry VI, Part II*, Margaret's love affair with the Duke of Suffolk comes into the open. (He is a married man as well; their situation is impossible.) Suffolk has arranged the murder of King Henry's uncle, the Duke of Gloucester, a political enemy. Gloucester is a highly respected and popular nobleman, Lord Protector of the realm during King Henry's long minority, and brother of the late, heroic King Henry V. But Suffolk's denial that he is in any way involved in the good duke's death falls on both deaf and unbelieving ears. The "Commons" (the people) demand Suffolk's death, but King Henry, gentle soul that he is, orders Suffolk into a lifetime of exile. Left alone in the palace chamber with Suffolk, Queen Margaret faces the inevitable and must bid a last farewell to the man she passionately loves and depends on.

QUEEN MARGARET

Enough, sweet Suffolk; thou torment'st thyself;
And these dread curses, like the sun 'gainst glass,
Or like an overcharged gun, recoil,
And turn the force of them upon thyself.
O, let me entreat thee cease. Give me thy hand,
That I may dew it with my mournful tears;
Nor let the rain of heaven wet this place,
To wash away my woeful monuments.
O, could this kiss be printed in thy hand,
That thou mightst think upon these by the seal,
Through whom a thousand sighs are breathed for thee!
So, get thee gone, that I may know my grief;
'Tis but surmised whiles thou art standing by,
As one that surfeits thinking on a want.
I will repeal thee, or, be well assured,
Adventure to be banished myself:
And banished I am, if but from thee.
Go: speak not to me; even now be gone.
O, go not yet! Even thus two friends condemn'd

Embrace and kiss and take ten thousand leaves,
Loather a hundred times to part than die.
Yet now farewell; and farewell life with thee!

King Henry VI, Part III
QUEEN MARGARET—ACT I, SCENE 1

AGE: Mature (Any age)   INTENT: Serious

Through the years of marriage and reigning, Margaret's
nerves have turned raw and she grows more and more
infuriated at her husband's incapacity to govern and to rule. At
the end of *King Henry VI, Part II*, the Yorkists have won the
Battle of St. Albans, and, for the time, have the secure upper
hand in the on-going War of the Roses. As a compromise, King
Henry agrees to make the Duke of York regent of the country,
with Henry to retain the titular title of king only for his
lifetime. Upon Henry's death, the crown would be inherited by
York and his heirs in perpetuity. Henry, in effect, agreed to
disinherit his own son, Edward, Prince of Wales, and his future
descendants. This action does not sit well with either the prince
nor Queen Margaret (and for good reason). This is the action
that drives Margaret into a final, revengeful fury that leads to
all but open rebellion against her husband and propels forward
the revenge-plot device of *King Henry VI, Part III*. (It would be
rebellion against Henry, except Margaret becomes head of the
Lancasterians against the Yorkists—i.e., fighting her husband's
battles for him to maintain her son's rights.)

   Here, Margaret has learned of King Henry's "compromise"
and confronts him. At no time, because of her fury and
indignation at this last incapacity of a king that ignites a
betrayal by husband and father, does she consider the appease-
ment and reasoning Henry tries to give for his actions.

QUEEN MARGARET

Nay, go not from me; I will follow thee.
Who can be patient in such extremes?
Ah, wretched man! would I had died a maid,
And never seen thee, never borne thee son,
Seeing thou has proved so unnatural a father!
Hath he deserved to lose his birthright thus?
Hadst thou but loved him half so well as I,
Or felt that pain which I did for him once,
Or nourish'd him as I did with my blood,
Thou wouldst have left thy dearest heart-blood there,
Rather than have made that savage duke thine heir
And disinherited thine only son.
        [A]rt thou king, and wilt be forced?
I shame to hear thee speak. Ah, timorous wretch!
Thou hast undone thyself, thy son and me;
And given unto the house of York such head
As thou shalt reign but by their sufferance.
To entail him and his heirs unto the crown,
What is it, but to make thy sepulchre
And creep into it far before thy time?
Warwick is chancellor and the lord of Calais;
Stern Falconbridge commands the narrow seas;
The duke is made protector of the realm;
And yet shalt thou be safe? Such safety finds
The trembling lamb environed with wolves.
Had I been there, which am a silly woman,
The soldiers should have toss'd me on their pikes
Before I would have granted to that act.
But thou preferr'st thy life before thine honour:
And seeing thou dost, I here divorce myself
Both from thy table, Henry, and thy bed,
Until that act of parliment be repeal'd
Whereby my son is disinherited.
The northern lords that have forsworn thy colours

Will follow mine, if once they see them spread;
And spread they shall be, to thy foul disgrace
And utter ruin of the house of York.
Thus do I leave thee. Come, son, let's away;
Our army is ready; come we'll after them.
           [Exit.]

King Richard III
LADY ANNE—ACT IV, SCENE 1

AGE: young (Any age)   INTENT: Serious

Among other things, Lady Anne is the widow of Edward, Prince of Wales (son of King Henry VI) whom Richard III helped murder after the battle of Tewkesbury, and she is the daughter of the Earl of Warwick ("the Kingmaker") whom the Yorkists fought and allowed to die unaided at the Battle of Barnet. (The two events happened within a mouth of each other.) Then, with great charm, Richard courted Anne and won her over. But by all indications the marriage (in the play) is anything but a successful one. Lady Anne soon regrets her actions and lives a life of fear, loathing, and misery.

Act IV, Scene 1 is Anne's penultimate appearance in the play. She is escorting her niece, Lady Margaret Plantagenet (the Duke of Clarence's daughter) to the Tower of London to visit the young princes. They meet Queen Elizabeth and the Duchess of York, also on their way to see the princes. The women are denied entry, upon Richard's order; and in the next breath Anne is summoned by Lord Stanley, Earl of Derby, to Westminster, "There to be crowned Richard's royal queen." Thus, altogether, do the women learn of Richard's ascension to the throne. And they all fear at once how he obtained the throne. Anne, reluctant queen, senses her own dire future as she goes as she is ordered, powerless to do otherwise.

LADY ANNE

Despiteful tidings! O unpleasing news!
And I in all unwillingness will go.
I would to God that the inclusive verge
Of golden metal that must round my brow
Were red-hot steel, to sear me to the brain!
Anointed let me be with deadly venom,
And die, ere men can say, God save the queen!
    When he that is my husband now
Came to me, as I follow'd Henry's corse,
When scarce the blood was well wash'd from his hands
Issued from my other angel husband
And that dead saint which then I weeping follow'd;
O, when, I say, I look'd on Richard's face,
This was my wish: "Be thou," quoth I, "accursed,
For making me, so young, so old a widow!
And, when thou wed'st, let sorrow haunt thy bed;
And be thy wife—if any be so mad—
As miserable by the life of thee
As thou hast made me by my dear lord's death!"
Lo, ere I can repeat this curse again,
Even in so short a space, my woman's heart
Grossly grew captive to his honey words
And proved the subject of my own soul's curse,
Which ever since hath kept my eyes from rest;
For never yet one hour in his bed
Have I enjoy'd the golden dew of sleep,
But have been waked by timorous dreams.
Besides, he hates me for my father Warwick,
And will, no doubt, shortly be rid of me.

King John
CONSTANCE—ACT III, SCENE 1

AGE: Any age   INTENT: Serious

Constance is another in Shakespeare's line of royal women who is betrayed by the men surrounding her, and upon whom she depends. Constance is the widow of Geoffery Plantagenet, younger brother of Richard I. Geoffery pre-deceased Richard, and in 1190 Richard named Geoffery's and Constance's son, Arthur, as his heir to the throne of England. Before Arthur, who is a minor, can claim the throne, his other uncle, John (Richard's youngest brother), produces a later will in which he is named heir over Arthur. Constance wages a continual struggle—by force if necessary by allying herself with France and Austria—to secure her son's rights and gain recognition to his claims to the English throne.

Armies from England and France have met before the city of Angiers. The battle results are inconclusive but the negotiated terms of peace are far from inconclusive. By terms of the truce, King John agrees to marry his niece, Blanch, to the French Dauphin, Lewis, and cede five rich provinces back to France as her dowry. In return France (and her allies) will withdraw their support to Arthur's claims to the English throne. Constance's reaction to all of this "trafficking and bargaining" is a forceful and natural resentment. She and her son have been betrayed for political expediency. Immediately after being informed of the terms of the treaty, Constance confronts King John, King Philip of France, and Lymoges, Duke of Austria, in the camp of the French.

CONSTANCE

What hath this day deserved? what hath it done,
That it in golden letters should be set
Among the high tides in the calendar?

Nay, rather turn this day out of the week,
This day of shame, opression, perjury,
Or, if it must stand still, let wives with child
Pray that their burthens may not fall this day,
Lest that their hopes prodigiously be cross'd:
But on this day let seamen fear no wreck;
No bargains break that are not this day made:
This day, all things begun come to ill end,
Yea, faith itself to hollow falsehood change!
You have beguiled me with a counterfeit
Resembling majesty, which, being touch'd and tried,
Proves valueless: you are forsworn, forsworn;
You came in arms to spill mine enemies blood,
But now in arms you strengthen it with yours:
The grappling vigour and rough frown of war
Is cold in amity and painted peace,
And our opression hath made up this league.
Arm, arm you heavens, against these perjured kings!
A widow cries: be husband to me, heavens!
Let not the hours of this ungodly day
Wear out the day in peace; but, ere sunset,
Set armed discord 'twixt these perjured kings!
Hear me, O, hear me!
War! War! no peace! peace is to me a war.
O Lymoges! O Austria! thou does shame
That bloody spoil; thou slave, thou wretch, thou coward!
Thou little valiant, great in villany!
Thou ever strong upon the stronger side!
Thou Fortune's champion that dost never fight
But when her humorous ladyship is by
To teach thee safety! thou are perjured too,
And soothest up greatness. What a fool art thou,
A ramping fool, to brag and stanp and swear
Upon my party! Thou cold-blodded slave,
Hath thou not spoke like thunder on my side,
Been sworn my soldier, bidding me depend

Upon my stars, thy fortune and thy strength,
And dost thou now fall over my foes?
Thou wear a lion's hide! doff it for shame,
And hang a calf's-skin on those recreant limbs.

King Henry IV, Part II
MISTRESS QUICKLY—ACT II, SCENE 1

AGE: Any age (Mature)   INTENT: Humorous

Mistress Quickly is the "hostess"/proprietress of the Boar's Head Tavern, Eastcheap. This tavern is also the headquarters of Sir John Falstaff and his coterie of dissolute followers. Mistress Quickly speaks plainly and bluntly, but the customers and inhabitants of her establishment are not persons who are managed by soft requests and genteel pleas. Mistress Quickly knows her world and its social order, and she complies as the needs of the occasion demand.

Sir John Falstaff owes Mistress Quickly a goodly sum of money, and to stave off paying her, he has made promises to marry her. However, neither money nor marriage have come forth; so, Mistress Quickly has entered an action in the courts and brought suit against Sir John for breach of both debts. After the proper legal complaints have been registered, Mistress Quickly accompanies two of the Sheriff's officers, Fang and Snare, on their quest to arrest Sir John and to see he's "brought to justice."

MISTRESS QUICKLY

Master Fang, have you entered the action? Where's your yeoman? Is't a lusty yeoman? will a' stand to't? Yea, good Master Snare; I have entered him and all. Alas, the day! take heed of him; he stabbed me in mine own house, and that most beastly: in good faith, he cares not what mischief he does, if his weapon be out: he will foin like any devil; he will spare neither

man, woman, nor child, I am undone by his going; I warrant
you, he's an infinitive thing upon my score. Good Master Fang,
hold him sure: good Master Snare, let him not 'scape. A'
comes continuantly to Piecorner—saving your manhoods—to
buy a saddle; and he is indited to dinner to the Lubber's-head
in Lumbert street, to Master Smooth's the silkman: I pray ye,
since my exion is entered and my case so openly known to the
world, let him be brought in to his answer. A hundred mark is a
long one for a poor lone woman to bear: and I have borne, and
borne, and borne, and have been fubbed off, and fubbed off,
and fubbed off, from this day to that day, that it is a shame to
be thought on. There is no honesty in such dealing; unless a
woman should be made an ass and a beast, to bear every
knave's wrong. Yonder he comes; and that arrant malmsey-
nose knave, Bardolph, with him. Do your offices, do your
offices: Master Fang and Master Snare, do me, do me, do me
your offices.

King Henry IV, Part II
DOLL TEARSHEET—ACT II, SCENE 4

AGE: Any age   INTENT: Humorous

Victorian writers, in their inestimable way of skirting the
sexually obvious, referred to Doll Tearsheet as "a low
woman." Another generation would have referred to her as "a
woman of easy virtue." Doll is one of those mainstays of
dramatic literature from over the centuries: a sympathetic
prostitute with a heart of gold. And in the Shakespearean world
she is also a woman of character and certain standards; she has
her price, but she also has her dignity and moral measures to
uphold and to protect. She insists on exerting what control she
can over her life and profession.
    Mistress Quickly, owner and hostess of the Boar's Head
Tavern in Eastcheap, has taken Doll under a sympathetic wing,
because Doll has become "sick of a calm" from drinking "Too

much canaries; and that's a marvellous searching win. . . ." Into
the tavern comes Sir John Falstaff and his retinue of
scoundrels, especially one Pistol, Sir John's "ancient" or
"ensign." Pistol suffers from that predominantly male point of
view that not only is he irresistible, but also that any woman is
an easy, capitulating conquest—especially a woman like Doll,
who has a notorious business reputation, as her name implies.
But Doll does not like Pistol, and she rejects and repels his
barrages of verbal innuendoes and lurid assaults. (N.B.—in
Elizabethan slang "charge" was usually equated with "to assail
sexually.")

DOLL TEARSHEET

Charge me! I scorn you, scurvy companion. What! you poor,
base, rascally, cheating, lack-linen mate! Away, you mouldy
rogue, away! I am meat for your master. Away, you cut-purse
rascal! you filthy bung, away! by this swine I'll thrust my knife
in your mouldy chaps, an you play the saucy cuttle with me.
Away, you bottle-ale rascal! you basket-hilt stale juggler, you!
Since when, I pray you, sir? God's light, with two points on
your shoulder? much! Captain! thou abominable damned
cheater, art thou not ashamed to be called captain? An captains
were of my mind, they would truncheon you out, for taking
their names upon you before you have earned them. You a
captain! you slave, for what? for tearing a poor whore's ruff in
a bawdy-house? He a captain! hang him, rogue! he lives upon
mouldy stewed prunes and dried cakes. A captain! God's light,
these villains will make the word as odious as the word
"occupy"; which was an excellent good word before it was ill
sorted: therefore captains had need to look to't. For God's sake,
thrust him down stairs; I cannot endure such a fustian rascal.

King Henry V
HOSTESS—ACT II, SCENE 3

AGE: Any age (Mature)   INTENT: Serious

Can a heart break? Can a person die of a broken heart? It just
might be possible. What we now clinically refer to as
"emotional trauma" can lead to physical ailments and break-
downs. After his public repudiation by King Henry V, Sir John
Falstaff contracted severe fevers and other ailments which
drained the life from him. To on-lookers, they may appear the
physical misfortunes of an old reprobate, but Mistress Quickly
(the Hostess) knows that "the king has killed his heart."

At the end of *King Henry IV, Part II*, Mistress Quickly was
in prison on a charge of mayhem, at least, if not possible
murder. Some time between then and the events of *King Henry
V*, she returns to her tavern in Eastcheap and has married Sir
John's ancient (ensign), Pistol. Sir John has also come to the
Boar's Head Tavern to die. Mistress Quickly nurses him to the
last. This "death of Falstaff" speech is both brief and moving in
its simplicity and its charm. What moved Mistress Quickly as
she experienced Falstaff's death is what also moves the
listeners, Pistol, Nym, and others of Sir John's crew, as the
they experience her reliving those last moments in Sir John's
life.

HOSTESS

Nay, sure, he's not in hell: he's in Arthur's bosom, if ever man
went to Arthur's bosom. A' made a finer end and went away an
it had been any christom child; a' parted even just between
twelve and one, even at the turning o' the tide; for after I saw
him fumble with the sheets and play with flowers and smile
upon his fingers' ends, I knew there was but one way; for his
nose was as sharp as a pen, and a' babbled of green fields.
"How now, Sir John!" quoth I: "what, man! be o' good cheer."

So a' cried out "God, God, God!" three or four times. Now I, to comfort him, bid him a' should not think of God; I hoped there was no need to trouble himself with any such thoughts yet. So a' bade me lay more clothes on his feet: I put my hand into the bed and felt them, and they were as cold as any stone, and so upward and upward, and all was as cold as any stone. For Falstaff he is dead, and we must yearn therefore.

King Henry VIII
QUEEN KATHERINE—ACT IV, SCENE 2

AGE: Mature (Any age)   INTENT: Serious

For nearly twenty-five years, Katherine of Aragon, daughter of Spain's Ferdinand and Isabella, was Queen Consort of England's King Henry VIII. Then she was divorced, annulled, and set aside with the title of Dowager Queen. Queen Katherine, as drawn by Shakespeare, is a proud and strong woman. She takes much pride in her birth and her marriage rank and she never waivers from her sense of her own station. Yet, mingled with these characteristics are qualities of long-enduring affection and a religious humility that blend to create a noble dignity and a gentle pathos of a woman wronged by circumstances. (Another royal woman betrayed by the man or men upon whom she most depends.) Queen Katherine uses these qualities to the very end in her struggle to maintain the position and the rank to which she feels she has the right.

Katherine as Dowager Queen is living in "genteel poverty" (for a queen). She is also in ill-health and she is dying. Her times is short and she knows it. Yet, there is much business to conclude concerning the welfare of her daughter, Mary, and her royal servants. This characteristic of Katherine's, thinking of others even at moments of personal pain and crisis, is what raises her from the merely unfortunate to the noble, dignified lady, wronged by circumstances over which she had no control—nor ever could have had. Katherine's final opportunity to

make her worries and wishes known to King Henry comes
when she receives a courtesy visit from Capucius, the Spanish
ambassador to the English court. (The Spanish king, the
Emperor Charles V, is also Katherine's nephew.) Katherine
seizes the opportunity to ask Capucius to be her emissary to
Henry. She uses her characteristic humility to ask the favor, but
underlying the request with regal urgency. In attendance to
Katherine, besides Capucius, are Katherine's gentleman-usher,
Griffith, and a lady-in-waiting, Patience.

QUEEN KATHERINE

    Patience, is that letter,
I caused you write, yet sent away?
Sir, I most humbly pray you to deliver
This to my lord the king.
In which I have commended to his goodness
The model of our chaste loves, his young daughter;
The dews of heaven fall thick in blessings on her!
Beseeching him to give her virtuous breeding,—
She is young, and of a noble modest nature,
I hope she will deserve well,—and a little
To love her for her mother's sake, that loved him,
Heaven knows how dearly. My next poor petition
Is, that his noble grace would have some pity
Upon my wretched women, that so long
Have follow'd both my fortunes faithfully:
Of which there is not one, I dare avow,
And now I should not lie, but will deserve,
For virtue and true beauty of the soul,
For honesty and decent carriage,
A right good husband, let him be a noble:
And, sure, those men are happy that shall have 'em.
The last is, for my men; they are the poorest,
But poverty could never draw 'em from me:
That they may have their wages duly paid 'em,

And something over to remember me by:
If heaven had pleased to have given me longer life
And able means, we had not parted thus.
These are the whole contents: and, good my lord,
But that you love the dearest in this world,
And you wish Christian peace to souls departed,
Stand these poor people's friend, and urge the king
To do me this last right. Remember me
In all humility unto his highness:
Say his long trouble now is passing
Out of this world; tell him, in death I bless'd him,
For so I will. Mine eyes grow dim. Farewell,
My lord. Griffith, farewell. Nay, Patience,
You must not leave me yet: I must to bed;
Call in more women. When I am dead, good wench,
Let me be used with honour: strew me over
With maiden flowers, that all the world may know
I was a chaste wife to my grave: embalm me,
Then lay me forth: although unqueen'd, yet like
A queen, and daughter to a king, inter me.
I can no more.
                              [Exit.]

PART II: THE COMEDIES

The Two Gentlemen of Verona
SILVIA—ACT IV, SCENE 3

AGE: Young   INTENT: Serious

This is one of Shakespeare's earliest comedies, and his first romantic comedy. Moreover, it is one in which he began experimenting with characters and situations that would come to fuller blossom in his later, more produced, and richer comedies. Silvia is the daughter of the reigning duke of Milan. She is daring and she is witty (something Shakespeare seemed to admire in women, and qualities with which he endowed most of his heroines). Silvia is also in love with Valentine, a young gentleman from Verona attached for the time to the ducal court in Milan. Valentine returns her love. However, her father, the Duke, has other plans for Silvia, which includes her betrothal to a foolish nobleman named Thurio. The Duke's good opinion of Valentine is further thwarted by Proteus, Valentine's best friend, who also has designs on Silvia. But Silvia remains true to Valentine. The Duke banishes Valentine from Milan for trying to elope with Silvia. Silvia, however, is determined to disobey her father's orders to marry Thurio, and she intends to follow after Valentine in a clandestine fashion

It is late at night, outside Silvia's chambers in the Duke's palace, and Silvia is meeting with another courtier, Sir Eglamour, whom she has asked to escort her to Mantua so she may be with her exiled love, Valentine.

SILVIA

Sir Eglamour, a thousand times good morrow.
O Eglamour, thou art a gentleman—
Think not I flatter, for I swear I do not—

Valiant wise, remorseful, well accomplish'd:
Thou art not ignorant what dear good will
I bear unto the banish'd Valentine,
Nor how my father would enforce me marry
Vain Thurio, whom my very soul abhors.
Thyself has loved; and I have heard thee say
No grief did ever come so near thy heart
As when thy lady and thy true love died,
Upon whose grave thou vow'dst pure chastity.
Sir Eglamour, I would to Valentine,
To Mantua, where I hear he makes abode;
And, for the ways are dangerous to pass,
I do desire thy worthy company,
Upon whose faith and honour I repose.
Urge not my father's anger, Eglamour,
But think upon my grief, a lady's grief,
And on the justice of my flying hence,
To keep me from a most unholy match,
Which heaven and fortune still rewards with plagues.
I do desire thee, even from a heart
As full of sorrows as the sea of sands,
To bear me company and go with me:
If not to hide what I have said to thee,
That I may venture to depart alone.
Good morrow, kind Sir Eglamour.
                    [Exeunt severally.]

The Two Gentleman of Verona
JULIA—ACT IV, SCENE 4

AGE: Young   INTENT: Serious

The role of Julia deserves a special footnote in the history of
Shakespeare's plays. She is the first of his famous
"breeches" roles. When Julia assumes the disguise of a male
page to follow after her lover, Proteus, Shakespeare began the

practice he was to use to great effect in later plays. Since woman's roles were played by adolescent boys and young men, it was very convincing, not to say practical, to have these boy-actors disguise themselves as boys!

Julia is a sweet and unselfish young woman who is in love with Proteus, a young man who, as the story progresses, turns into a treacherous and unpleasant twerp. He turns his affections from Julia once he sees Silvia, who is in love with his best friend, Valentine. And Proteus then plots to steal Silvia from Valentine. But this doesn't deter Julia. In a situation that foreshadows the Viola-Orsino relationship in *Twelfth Night*, Julia courts Silvia as a male page for Proteus. Of course, she is so convincing as a boy that Proteus does not recognize her as the lady he left behind in Verona, nor does Silvia suspect that Julia is another female, let alone the hapless Julia herself.

Julia, in disguise, has just had an interview with Silvia, an interview that has surprised Julia. As the page, she has brought a letter to Silvia from Proteus, along with the gift of a ring, the very ring which Julia herself gave Proteus as a token when he left Verona. Silvia knows about Proteus' jilting of Julia, and she rejects both Proteus' written protestations and the ring, saying that while Proteus' "false finger have profaned the ring, /Mine shall not do his Julia so much wrong." Silvia has just left the sorrowing and disguised Julia alone with her reactions to this unusual and unexpected encounter.

JULIA

A virtuous gentlewoman, mild and beautiful!
I hope my master's suit will be but cold,
Since she respects my mistress' love so much.
Alas, how love can trifle with itself!
Here is her picture: let me see; I think,
If I had such a tire, this face of mine
Were full as lovely as is this of hers:
And yet the painter flatter'd her a little,

Unless I flatter with myself too much.
Her hair is auburn, mine is perfect yellow:
If that be all the difference in his love,
I'll get me such a colour'd periwig.
Her eyes are grey as glass, and so are mine:
Ay, but her forehead's low, and mine's high.
What should it be that he respects in her
But I can make respective in myself,
If this fond Love were not a blinded god?
Come, shadow, come, and take this shadow up,
For 'tis thy rival. O thou senseless form,
Thou shalt be worshipp'd, kiss'd, loved and adored!
And, were there sense in his idolatry,
My substance should be statue in thy stead.
I'll use thee kindly for thy mistress' sake,
That used me so; or else, by Jove I vow,
I should have scratch'd out your unseeing eyes,
To make my master out of love with thee!
[Exit.]

The Taming of the Shrew
KATHARINA—ACT VI, SCENE 3

AGE: Young (Any age)   INTENT: Humorous

Kate and Petruchio are Shakespeare's first pair of unforgettable comic lovers, creations that entered into the lexicons as named examples of such relationships. Shakespeare had an outstanding sympathy with his women characters, and an almost uncanny understanding of them. It is one of the distinguishing features of his plays—especially of his comedies. But it must also be remembered that Shakespeare's moral outlook was always conformist and conservative. He was a normal family man (as much as his profession would allow him, with his family safely in Stratford), and his view was that of the normal Elizabethan one. And the normal Elizabethan view was that as dictated by St. Paul and as interpreted by the Church of the time: women were to be subject to their husbands, for the husband was the head of the woman.

The originality of this farce is that Petruchio "tames" his shrewish wife by comic means. They are outwardly rough, but mitigated by an inward love, for Petruchio really does love Katharina. (It is interesting to note that from the text of the play, Petruchio never strikes Kate, nor beats her, even though she slaps him.) Kate is to be tamed in comic terms. She is to be bridled, like a spring colt, with firmness mixed with unmitigated love. The twist is, of course, that Kate falls in love with her husband, but she is too proud and too obstinate to admit it.

Katharina has been compared to a wasp. She is pert; she is quick; she is determined. And underneath all of her petticoats she may have—and she should have—a good heart, or the audience would lose all care for her. By Act IV, Petruchio's system of taming his wife is starting to show its effects. Kate has not been allowed to rest nor has she had a full mean since she has left her father's house and arrived at Petruchio's villa. She is at the point of exhaustion from frustration—a comic victim of the mistress killed with kindness, so to speak. At the moment, Kate is trying to persuade Petruchio's servant, Grumio, by any means, to bring her some food. She is starving.

KATHARINA

The more my wrong, the more his spite appears:
What, did he marry me to famish me?
Beggars, that come into my father's door,
Upon entreaty have a present alms;
If not, elsewhere they meet with chairty:
But I, who never knew how to entreat,
Nor never needed that I should entreat,
Am starved for meat, giddy for lack of sleep,
With oaths kept waking and with brawling fed:

And that which spites me more than all these wants,
He does it under the name of perfect love;
And who should say, if I should sleep or eat,
'Twere deadly sickness or else present death.
I prithee go and get me some repast;
I care not what, so it be some wholesome food.

Love's Labour's Lost
PRINCESS OF FRANCE—ACT V, SCENE 2

AGE: Young   INTENT: Serious

Love's Labour's Lost is, perhaps, Shakespeare's most acutely personal play; and in it one finds his high spirits and examples of his verbal cleverness. One also finds the themes, situations, and characters he would use again and again and develop into greater roundness in his later plays, especially his romantic comedies. It is also a romantic comedy that mixes scenes of pure farce with scenes of intricate poetry and lyrical verse. And with this play, Shakespeare also experimented with closing a comedy of light-hearted gaiety with an ending of a rather somber note, though it also points toward a happy future.

The Princess of France is one of Shakespeare's most exquisite young female creations: right royal, quick and witty, and with her ladies, filled with drollery and full of mischief. She is a good match for the young King of Navarre. The "courtship" of the Princess and her three ladies by the King and his three companions (or it could be vice versa from another angle when viewed from behind the convenient tree) is the main action of the play. The courtship antics come to full fruition when the King and his companions come to the ladies' pavilion in the guise of rough and cumbersome "Muscovites." They are unmasked by the knowing ladies, who are aware of their plot, and each gentleman makes his proper protestations and proposal of marriage to his chosen lady. The romance and hope for a quadruple wedding ceremony are cut short,

however, when word arrives, quite unexpectedly, of the death
of the King of France. The gaiety of the play suddenly takes on
a somber and subdued mood. And while the Princess realizes
she loves the King of Navarre, the duties of grieving daughter
and princess must take precedence over personal wants and
wishes.

PRINCESS

I thank you, gracious lords,
For all your fair endeavors; and entreat,
Out of a new-sad soul, that you vouchsafe
In your rich wisdom to excuse or hide
The liberal opposition of your spirits,
If over-boldly we have borne ourselves
In the converse of breath: your gentleness
Was guilty of it. Farewell, worthy lord!
A heavy heart bears not a nimble tongue:
Excuse me so, coming too short of thanks
For my great suit so easily obtain'd.
We received your letters full of love;
Your favours, the ambassadors of love;
And, in our maiden council, rated them
At courtship, pleasant jest and courtesy,
As bombast and as lining to the time:
But more devout than this in our respects
Have we not been; and therefore met your loves
In their own fashion, like a merriment.
No, no, my lord, your grace is perjured much,
Full of dear guiltiness; and therefore this:
If for my love, as there is no such cause,
You will do aught, this shall you do for me:
Your oath I will not trust; but go with speed
To some forlorn and naked hermitage,
Remote from all the pleasures of the world;
There stay until the twelve celestial signs

Have brought about the annual reckoning.
If this austere insociable life
Change not your offer made in heat of blood;
It frosts and fasts, hard lodging and thin weeds
Nip not the gaudy blossoms of your love,
But that it bear this trial and last love;
Then, at the expiration of the year,
Come challenge me, challenge me by these deserts,
And by this virgin palm now kissing thine,
I will be thine; and till that instant shut
My woeful self up in a mourning house,
Raining the tears of lamentation
For the remembrance of my father's death.
If this thou do deny, let our hands part,
Neither entitled in the other's heart.

A Midsummer Night's Dream
TITANIA— ACT II, SCENE 1

AGE: Any age (Young)   INTENT: Humorous

One of Shakespeare's ever enduring influences upon Western literature was his evolution of the world of the "faerie." It is with the creation of Oberon and Titania that the fairies in English folklore become benevolent and, with his Puck, that they become mischievous with sprightly hearts whose blessings could lead to welcomed benefits and not malevolent spirits bent upon punishment and confusion amongst mortals and humanity. In *A Midsummer Night's Dream* Shakespeare created a fairy folk that humans need not fear, but a people that mere mortals wanted to see, to experience, to know; a fairy court to attend and from which humans wanted to receive blessings and attentions.

But all is not well in the dales and mists of the fairy kingdoms. It's twin monarchs, Oberon and Titania, are at odds with one another. They are arguing over the guardianship of a

young human boy, a changling, whom Oberon wants as his
page, and whom Titania is determined to keep in her circle because his mother was a "votaress of [her] order," though
mortal, and died giving birth to he boy. Titania has sworn to
avoid Oberon's company (and his bed) until he agrees to let
her keep the child. He is just as determined to capture the boy
for his own retinue. The two fairy monarchs and their
entourages meet unexpectedly in the forests outside of Athens
on St. John's Eve—mid-summer's eve—one of the most
magical nights of the year. They have come by their individual
paths to witness and to bless the marriage of Theseus, Duke of
Athens, to Hippolyta, Queen of the Amazons.

TITANIA

What, jealous Oberon! Fairies, skip hence:
I have forsworn his bed and company.
And never, since the middle summer's spring,
Met we on hill, in dale, forest or mead,
By paved fountain or by rushy brook,
Or in the beached margent of the sea,
To dance our ringlets to the whistling wind,
But with thy brawls thou hast disturb'd our sport.
Therefore the winds, piping to us in vain,
As in revenge, have suck'd up from the sea
Contagious fogs; which falling in the land
Have every pelting river made so proud
That they have overborne their continents:
The ox hath therefore stretch'd his yoke in vain,
The ploughman lost his sweat, and the green corn
Hath rotted ere his youth attain'd a beard;
The fold stands empty in the drowned field,
And crows are fatted with the murrion flock;
The nine men's morris is fill'd up with mud,
And the quaint mazes in the wanton green
For lack of tread are undistinguishable:

The human mortals want their winter here;
No night is now with hymn or carol blest:
Therefore the moon, the governess of floods,
Pale in her anger, washes all the air,
That rheumatic diseases do abound:
And through this distemperature we see
The seasons alter: hoary-headed frosts
Fall in the fresh lap of the crimson rose,
And on old Hiems' thin and icy crown
An odorous chaplet of sweet summer buds
Is, as in mockery, set: the spring, the summer,
The chilling autumn, angry winter, change
Their wonted liveries, and the mazed world,
By their increase, now knows not which is which:
And this same progeny of evils comes
From our debate, from our dissension;
We are their parents and original.
The fairy land buys not the child of me.
His mother was a votaress of my order:
And, in the spiced Indian air, by night,
Full often hath she gossip'd by my side,
And sat with me on Neptune's yellow sands,
Marking the embarked traders on the flood,
When we have laugh'd to see the sails conceive
And grow big-bellied with the wanton wind:
Which she, with pretty and with swimming gait
Following,—her womb then rich with my young squire,—
Would imitate, and sail upon the land,
To fetch me trifles, and return again,
As from a voyage, rich with merchandise.
But she, being mortal, of that boy did die;
And for her sake do I rear up her boy,
And for her sake I will not part with him.

As You Like It
ROSALIND—ACT III, SCENE 2

AGE: Young   INTENT: Humorous

One of the two most famous "breeches" parts in Shakespeare is Rosalind, daughter of the banished Duke, rightful ruler of the unnamed dominions where the Forest of Arden is located. And what a heroine of a play that is pure romantic comedy is Rosalind. She is a woman who is secure in who she is, even though circumstances which surround her may cause her trouble. She bubbles with wit, and she sparkles with spirit. She dances to the melodies of life. Her heart is an overflowing fountain that washes life and love and joy onto the people surrounding her. She is as fresh and as exhilarating as a sunny, warm day after a month of gray, rainy, cold winter weather.

Rosalind has been driven from the ducal court by her usurping uncle. She has been accompanied into banishment by her cousin, Celia, and the court clown, Touchstone. They have taken refuge, as does nearly everyone in the play, in the idyllic forest of Arden. There, Rosalind dons male clothing and assumes the name Ganymede, a young shepherd, living with his sister, Aliena (Celia). Also wandering through the forest is Orlando, driven from his home by his older brother. Orlando saw Rosalind when at court and he fell in love with her at first sight. He has been meandering through the forest tacking love poems and epistles to his beloved Rosalind on numerous trees. Rosalind, of course, also loves Orlando. But since she is in the guise of a boy, she can't declare her acceptance of his attentions very well.

Rosalind overhears Orlando confess his passion for her to the melancholy Jacques, and decides to "Speak to [Orlando] like a saucy lackey and under the habit play the knave with him." In that way, Rosalind hatches a scheme of how she may keep company with Orlando without foregoing her alias.

ROSALIND

There is none of my uncle's marks upon you: he taught me how to know a man in love; in which cage of rushes I am sure you are not prisoner. A lean cheek, which you have not, a blue eye and sunken, which you have not, an unquestionable spirit, which you have not, a beard neglected, which you have not; but I pardon you for that, for simply your having in beard is a younger brother's revenue: then your hose should be ungartered, your bonet unbanded, your sleeve unbuttoned, your shoe untied and every thing about you demonstrating a careless desolation; but you are no such man; you are rather point-device in your accoutrements as loving yourself than seeming the lover of any other. But, in good sooth, are you he that hangs the verses on the trees, wherein Rosalind is so admired? Are you so much in love as your rhymes speak? Love is merely a madness, and, I tell you, deserves as well a dark house and a whip as madmen do: and the reason why they are not so punished and cured is, that the lunacy is so ordinary that the whippers are in love too. Yet I profess curing it by counsel [such a one], and in this manner. He was to imagine me his love, his mistress; and I set him every day to woo me: at which time would I, being but a moonish youth, grieve, be effeminate, changeable, longing and liking, proud, fantastical, apish, shallow, inconstant, full of tears, full of smiles, for every passion something and for no passion truly any thing, as boys and women are for the most part cattle of this colour; would now like him, now loathe him; then entertain him, then forswear him; now weep for him, then spit at him; that I drave my suitor from his mad humor of love to a living humour of madness; which was, to forswear the full stream of the world and to live in a nook merely monastic. And thus I cured him; and this way will I take upon me to wash your liver as clean as a sound sheep's heart, that there shall not be one spot of love in't.

As You Like It
PHEBE—ACT III, SCENE 5

AGE: Young   INTENT: Humorous

Phebe is quite a country coquette. She is referred to as an
Arcadian beauty, and she is described as having inky
brows, black silk hair, bugle eyeballs, and cheeks of cream.
Phebe is loved by Silvius, a young shepherd who is both
humble and long-suffering. Nothing Phebe does can repel his
attention nor stave off his ardor, both of which Phebe likes
when she needs them. But Phebe has spotted Ganymede
(Rosalind) and has focused her inconstant amorous attentions
on "him," much to Ganymede's dismay. Rosalind tries
immediately to squelch Phebe's hopes and advances, but Phebe
is a girl who, once her mind is set, takes a sturdy "no" as a
definite "maybe." She also uses her wiles to keep the shepherd
she already has in her pen. She does not like to be rejected—
the attentions from a male have probably never walked away
from her before this moment. It's quite a new and unpleasant
experience for her.

PHEBE

Know'st thou the youth that spoke to me erewhile?
Think not I love him, though I ask for him;
'Tis but a peevish boy; yet he talks well;
But what care I for words? yet words do well
When he that speaks them pleases those that hear.
It is a pretty youth: not very pretty:
But, sure, he's proud, and yet his pride becomes him:
He'll make a proper man: the best thing in him
Is his complexion; and faster than his tongue
Did make offence his eye did heal it up.
He is not very tall; yet for his years he's tall:
His leg is but so so; and yet 'tis well:

ere was a pretty redness in his lip,
A little riper and more lusty red
Than that mix'd in his cheek; 'twas just the difference
Betwixt the constant red and mingled damask.
There be some women, Silvius, had they mark'd him
In parcels as I did, would have gone near
To fall in love with him; but, for my part,
I love him not nor hate him not; and yet
I have more cause to hate him than to love him:
For what had he to do to chide at me?
He said mine eyes were black and my hair black:
And, now I am remember'd, scorn'd at me:
I marvel why I answered not again:
But that's all one; omittance is no quittance.
I'll write him a very taunting letter,
The matter's in my head and in my heart;
I will be bitter with him and passing short.
And thou shall bear it, Silvus. Go with me.
                    [Exit.]

The Merry Wives of Windsor
MISTRESS QUICKLY—ACT II, SCENE 2

AGE: Mature (Any age)   INTENT: Humorous

The last play Shakespeare composed containing Sir John
Falstaff, *The Merry Wives of Windsor*, is a farce centered
on the antics of the middle-class from which Shakespeare
sprang. This time Mistress Quickly, who seems to be paired
with Falstaff in the way Margaret Dumont is with Groucho
Marx, is the respectable housekeeper of one Dr. Caius, a
French Physician who murders the language in broken English.
But Mistress Quickly has not changed her spots all that much.
This Mistress Quickly, while having been given a larger part in
the intrigues against Sir John, is still inclined to be as much of

a bawd as ever—just as is the Mistress Quickly, hostess of the
Boar's Head Tavern in Eastcheap.

Mistress Quickly is something of an emissary and go-
between, a connection amongst all the intrigues that make up
this play's plot. She is engaged by the foolish Slender and his
ninny friends to help in his romantic pursuit of the lovely Anne
Page. As a result, Mistress Quickly comes into contact with the
Mistresses Ford and Page who use her as a vessel to convey
their messages to the garrulous Sir John as part of their plot to
entrap and humiliate him for his grandiose romantic affronts he
has tendered to them. Having agreed to become part of the in-
trigue, Mistress Quickly comes to the Garter Inn to entice the
credulous Falstaff with promissory messages from Mistress
Ford and Mistress Page, co-objects of the fat knight's present
amours.

MISTRESS QUICKLY

Give your worship good morrow. Shall I vouchsafe your
worship a word of two? There is one Mistress Ford, sir:— I
pray, come a little nearer this ways:—I myself dwell with
Master Doctor Caius,—I pray your worship, come a little
nearer this ways. Why, sir, [Mistress Ford's] a good creature.
Lord, Lord! your worship's a wanton! Well, heaven forgive
you and all of us, I pray! Marry, this is the short and the long of
it; you have brought her into such a canaries as 'tis wonderful.
The best courtier of them all, when the court lay at Windsor,
could never have brought her to such a canary. Yet there has
been knights, and lords, and gentlemen, with their coaches, I
warrant you, coach after coach, letter after letter, gift after gift;
smelling so sweetly, all musk, and so rushing, I warrant you, in
silk and gold; and in such alligant terms; and in such wine and
sugar of the best and the fairest, that would have won any
woman's heart; and, I warrant you, they could never get an
eye-wink of her: I had myself twenty angels given me this
morning; but I defy all angels, in any such sort, as they say, but

in the way of honesty: and, I warrant you, they could never get her so much as sip on a cup with the proudest of them all: and yet there has been earls, nay, which is more, pensioners; but, I warrant you, all is one with her. Marry, she hath received your letter for which she thanks you a thousand times; and she gives you to notify that her husband will be absence from his house between ten and eleven. and then you may come and see the picture, she says, that you wot of: Master Ford, her husband, will be from home. Alas! the sweet woman leads a ill life with him: he's a very jealous man: she leads a very frampold life with him. But I have another messenger to your worship. Mistress Page hath her hearty commendations to you too: and let me tell you in your ear, she's as fartuous a civil modest wife, and one, I tell you, that will not miss you morning nor evening prayer, as any is in Windsor, whoe'er be the other; and she bade me tell your worship that her husband is seldom from home; but she hopes there will come a time. I never knew a woman so dote upon a man: surely I think you have charms, la; yes, in truth. But Mistress Page would desire you to send her your little page, of all loves; her husband has a marvelous infection to the little page; and truly Master Page is an honest man. Never a wife in Windsor leads a better life than she does: do what she will, say what she will, take all, pay all, go to bed when she list, rise when she list, all is as she will: and truly she deserves it; for if there be a kind woman in Windsor, she is one. You must send her your page; no remedy. [Do] so then: and, look you, he may come and go between you both; and in any case have a nay-word, that you may know one another's mind, and the boy never need to understand any thing; for 'tis not good that children should know any wickedness: old folks, you know have discretion, as they say, and know the world.

PART III: THE TRAGEDIES

Titus Andronicus
TAMORA—ACT III, SCENE 3

AGE: Mature (Any age)   INTENT: Serious

Titus Andronicus is Shakespeare's first tragedy. He wrote it very early in his career, and he tried to pour a little bit of everything into it, both to gain the notice and to please the tastes of the public, and also to outdo his contemporaries. And this play nearly has it all: rape and mutilation, madness, mayhem, betrayal, murder, revenge, interracial love affairs, and a cannibal banquet. It made dynamic theater for early Elizabethan stage, and it was a popular play in Shakespeare's day.

Tamora, queen of the Goths, is a thoroughly wicked, vile, self-effacing woman. She is one of the most singularly driven women created by Shakespeare. She is the motor that drives the revenge-plot forward throughout the play. She swears vengeance on Titus after he refuses her pleas and sacrifices her eldest son to avenge his own sons' deaths in the Gothic wars. Tamora gulls the Roman Emperor, Saturnius, into marrying her while she continues her passionate love affair with the other recalcitrant and remorseless villain of the play, Aaron the Moor. Together they arrange for Tamora's remaining two sons to rape Titus' daughter, Lavina, and then cut out her tongue and cut off her hands so she can never tell the story of what happened to her. They murder Lavina's husband and arrange that two of Titus's sons are blamed and executed for the deed. And, finally, at a banquet given by Titus, before he does her in, Tamora is fed a fresh pie containing the meat of the bodies of her two sons as the main dish of the meal.

Somewhat improbably in all of this, Tamora finds time to be romantic and wax lovingly about the peaceful countryside. This lyric evocation of the countryside and "romantic" love occurs in a scene between Tamora and Aaron in a "lonely part of the forest." outside Rome. While the speech evokes the idea that Tamora does have a passion for Aaron, a sequence like this also works within the framework of the play as a rest does in a musical score. It is a short breathing space for the audience before the crescendo of violent blood baths which pour over them immediately following.

TAMORA

My lovely Aaron, wherefore look'st thou sad,
When every thing doth make a gleeful boast?
The birds chant melody on every bush,
The snake lies rolled in the cheerful sun,
The green leaves quiver with the cooling wind
And make a chequer'd shadow on the ground:
Under their sweet shade, Aaron, let us sit,
And, whilst the babbling echo mocks the hounds,
Replying shrilly to the well-tuned horns,
As if a double hunt were heard at once,
Let us sit down and mark their yelping noise;
And, after conflict such as was supposed
The wandering prince and Dido once enjoy'd,
When with the happy storm they were surprised
And curtain'd with a counsel-keeping cave,
We may, each wreathed in the other's arms,
Our pastimes done, possess a golden slumber;
Whiles hounds and horns and sweet melodious birds
Be unto us as is a nurse's song
Of lullaby to bring her babe asleep.
Ah, my sweet Moor, sweeter to me than life!

Romeo and Juilet
JULIET'S NURSE—ACT I, SCENE 3

Age: Mature   INTENT: Humorous

Juliet's Nurse is a marvelous, down-to-earth woman, pragmatic about life, devoted to the Capulets, and most of all, dotes on her charge, Juliet. She is from sturdy peasant stock—probably from the country at one time. She is at turns garrulous and coarse, supportive and then deceitful, and she serves the circumstances of the times. At first she supports Juliet's secret marriage to Romeo; and once he is banished, she encourages the girl to forget that marriage as if it didn't happen and to accept the suit of Count Paris. The Nurse acts on the assumption that Romeo will never show up in Verona again. That about-face proposal reveals, more than any other, the deeply rooted base of the Nurse.

Lady Capulet has come to her daughter to inform her that Count Paris "seeks you for his love." But before Lady Capulet announces the news to Juliet, she has asked the Nurse confirmation of the girl's age. All the Nurse needs is a chink of an opening, and she is ready with a barrage of words and stories to support and illustrate her answer. The Nurse takes a hundred words to answer a question where only one or two are needed.

NURSE

Faith, I can tell her age unto an hour.
Come Lammas-eve at night shall she be fourteen.
Susan and she—God rest all Christian souls!—
Were of an age: well, Susan is with God;
She was too good for me: but, as I said,
On Lammas-eve at night shall she be fourteen;
That shall she, marry; I remember it well.
'Tis since the earthquake now eleven years;
And she was wean'd,—I never shall forget it,—

Of all the days of the year, upon that day:
For I had then laid wormwood to my dug,
Sitting in the sun under the dove-house wall;
My lord and you were then at Mantua:—
Nay, I do bear a brain:—but, as I said,
When it did taste the wormwood on the nipple
Of my dug and felt it bitter, pretty fool,
To see it tetchy and fall out with the dug!
"Shake" quoth the dove-house: 'twas no need, I trow,
To bid me trudge:
And since that time it is eleven years;
For then she could stand alone; nay, by the rood,
She could have run and waddled all about;
For even the day before, she broke her brow:
And then my husband—God be with his soul!
A' was a merry man—took up the child:
"Yea," quoth he, "dost thou fall upon thy face?
Thou wilt fall backward when thou has more wit;
Wilt thou not, Jule?" and, by my holidame,
The pretty wretch left crying and said "Ay."
To see, now, how jest shall come about!
I warrant, an I should live a thousand years,
I never should forget it: "Wilt thou not, Jule?" quoth he;
And, pretty fool, it stinted and said "Ay."
Yes, madam: yet I cannot choose but laugh,
To think it should leave crying and say "Ay."
And yet, I warrant, it had upon its brow
A bump as big as a young cockerel's stone;
A parlous knock; and it cried bitterly:
"Yea," quoth my husband, "fall'st upon thy face?
Thou wilt fall backward when thou comest to age;
Wilt thou not, Jule?" it stinted and said "Ay."
Peace, I have done. God mark thee to his grace!
Thou wast the prettiest babe that e're I nursed:
And I might live to see thee married once,
I have my wish.

Hamlet
OPHELIA—ACT III, SCENE 1

AGE: Young   INTENT: Serious

Ah! The Fair Ophelia! Is she noble and naive, or a pawn and
a dupe, or is she just plain stupid? That she is in love with
Hamlet there is no doubt. That Hamlet has at least lead Ophelia
to believe her love is returned from him, there is no doubt; and
it can be interpreted from statements made by Hamlet late in
the play that his love for her was true. And in contrast to
Laertes' warning to his sister that Hamlet's station does no
allow him to give his promises freely, Gertrude's lament over
Ophelia's grave that she had hoped the girl would have been
sweet Hamlet's wife shows that Ophelia was of rank high
enough to be considered seriously as a future queen.

Hamlet's most bitter words in the play are to Ophelia. Why?
Is it for the reason psychology would tell us: that at moments
of soul rendering, when a person is being shredded in two,
there is the desire to mortify and to destroy the person one
loves most? Or is it from Hamlet's awareness of the intrigues
which surround him, and he is vicious to the girl simply to protect her from danger? Or does he truly believe she is another
who has betrayed him? For whatever the reason, Ophelia has
just experienced a biting and confounding encounter with the
man she deeply loves, and with the man who, always before,
had been solicitous and considerate to her. Now she is deserted,
alone, and she bleeds.

OPHELIA

O, what a noble mind is here o'erthrown!
The courtier's, soldier's, scholar's, eye, tongue, sword;
The expectancy and rose of the fair state,
The glass of fashion and the mould of form,
The observed of all observers, quite, quite down!

And I, of ladies most deject and wretched,
That suck'd the honey of his music vows,
Now see that noble and most sovereign reason,
Like sweet balls jangled, out of tune and harsh;
That unmatch'd form and feature of blown youth
Blasted with ecstasy: O, woe is me,
To have seen what I have seen, see what I see!

Macbeth
LADY MACBETH—ACT I, SCENE 5

AGE: Any Age (Mature)   INTENT: Serious

Sometimes one of the hardest assignments an actor has in a
play is the reading of a letter. If one aspect of acting is
physicalizing emotions through words, letter reading on stage
sometimes becomes an exercise in recitation without thought to
the purpose other than information. Such is the case with Lady
Macbeth's first appearance in the play: she is reading a letter
reiterating events the audience already knows—unless it was
put in to inform the latecomers. And since, too, this is the
audience's introduction to Lady Macbeth, the actress has to
consider seriously a number of choices about background and
"backstory" knowledge before she steps into the stage lights. Is
this the first time Lady Macbeth has read the letter, or it this
several times later? Is Lady Macbeth surprised at what the
letter reveals and is she planning spontaneously; or is this
reading a search for confirmation and support of schemes
already formulating? How well does Lady Macbeth know her
husband? his dreams? his ambitions? Have they, on long
Scottish winter nights, before the fire and over cups of grog,
speculated on how the seize the crown for themselves?
Contemplated murder? How to contrive an opportunity to
eliminate Duncan? Or is Lady Macbeth "shooting from the
hip"? All of the choices the actress implements on this first

entrance of the Lady will direct the growth and path of the role
to the heart rendering sleepwalking scene.

LADY MACBETH

[Enter LADY MACBETH, reading a letter.]
'They met me in the day of success; and I have learned by
the perfectest report, they have more in them than mortal
knowledge. When I burned in desire to question them further,
they made themselves air, into which they vanished. Whiles
I stood rapt in the wonder of it, came missives from the
king, who all-hailed me "Thane of Cawdor"; by which title,
before, the weird sisters saluted me, and referred me
 to the coming of time, with "Hail, king that shalt be!"
This I have thought good to deliver thee, my dearest partner
of greatness, that thou mightst not lose the dues of rejoicing,
by being ignorant of what greatness is promised thee. Lay
it to thy heart, and farewell.'
Glamis thou art, and Cawdor; and shall be
What thou art promised: yet I do fear thy nature;
It is too full o' the milk of human kindness
To catch the nearest way: thou wouldst be great;
Art not without ambition, but without
The illness should attend it; what thou wouldst highly,
That wouldst thou holily; wouldst not play false,
And yet wouldst wrongly win: thou'ldst have, great Glamis,
That which cries 'Thus thou must do, if thou have it;
And that which rather thou doest fear to do
Than wishest should be undone.' Hie thee hither,
That I may pour my spirits in thine ear;
And chastise with the valour of my tongue
All that impedes thee from the golden round,
Which fate and metaphysical aid doth seem
To have crown'd withal.

King Lear
GONERIL—ACT I, SCENE 3

AGE: Any age   INTENT: Serious

"**H**ow sharper than a serpent's tooth it is/To have a thankless child!" King Lear directs this famous pronouncement to his daughter, Goneril. Even though Lear is a foolish old man, who gives away all he has, and then expects gratitude, in this instance he does give an accurate insight into Goneril. Goneril is a formidable gorgon with a heart of stone who will annihilate anyone or anything that is an obstacle in her path. There is not much good that can be said about the woman, if any: she betrays her father, cuckholds her husband, poisons her collaborating sister, and conspires to the murders of her father and youngest sister (and probably would have murdered her own husband had she not committed suicide). If single-will and determination on a direct course are counted as virtues, then Goneril's virtues have been catalogued.

Goneril unfurls her true colors early in the play. Once she gets control of half of the kingdom, she wastes no time in letting everyone else know who is in charge. King Lear has barely retired from the throne before Goneril wants to set him down from the head table to "below the salt." She is going over the situation in her palace with her steward, Oswald.

GONERIL

Did my father strike my gentleman for chiding of his fool?
By day and night he wrongs me; every hour
He flashes into one gross crime or other,
That sets us all at odds: I'll not endure it:
His knights grow riotous, and himself upbraids us
On every trifle. When he returns from hunting,
I will not speak to him; say I am sick:
If you come slack of former services,

You shall do well: the fault of it I'll answer.
Put on what weary negligence you please,
You and your fellows; I'ld have it come to question:
If he dislike it, let him to our sister,
Whose mind and mine, I know, in that are one,
Not to be over-ruled. Idle old man,
That still would manage those authorities
That he hath given away! Now, by my life,
Old fools are babes again; and must be used
With checks and flatteries,—when they are seen abused.
Remember what I tell you.
And let his knights have colder looks among you;
What grows of it, no matter; advise your fellows so:
I would breed from hence occasions, and I shall,
That I may speak: I'll write straight to my sister,
To hold my very course. Prepare for dinner.
                    [Exit.]

King Lear
CORDELIA—ACT IV, SCENE 7

AGE: Young (Any age)   INTENT: Serious

Juliet, Ophelia, Cordelia. This trio of heroines seem to spark
the imaginations and ambitions of more young actresses than
any of the other female roles from the tragedies. The mistake
many young players make, however, in portraying these
women is that they mistake Cordelia's tenderness and care for
passivity and weakness. But Cordelia is a very strong character,
and this strength is derived from her honesty. Cordelia is one of
these people whose real feeling are too deep for words.
Unfortunately, early in her story, glib words are what are desired and are what carry the day.

    After being disowned by her father, King Lear, Cordelia is
married—without dowry—to the King of France and becomes
that country's queen. Cordelia is a woman who solicits great

devotion from the men around her: the Duke of Gloucester and his son, Edgar; the disgraced Earl of Kent, never waivers from his belief in her; and her husband creates an invasion force to accompany her back to Britain to save her father. And Cordelia, of course, epitomizes filial loyalty and love: through all her troubles she never slides from her love for her father.

The mad King Lear has been found by members of Cordelia's invasion force in the fields near Dover and they have brought him to the French camp, after a chase to catch him. Lear now sleeps, and Cordelia, the doctors, and the still disguised Kent are in attendance awaiting his revival with the hope that when he awakes he will have regained his wits. Cordelia verbalizes her emotions about the circumstances of her fallen father in a most intimate and private of moments.

CORDELIA

O you kind gods,
Cure this great breach in his abused nature!
The untuned and jarring senses, O, wind up
Of this child-changed father!
O my dear father! Restoration hang
Thy medicine on my lips; and let this kiss
Repair those violent harms that my two sisters
Have in thy reverence made!
Had you not been their father, these white flakes
Had challenged pity of them. Was this a face
To be opposed against the warring winds?
To stand against the deep dread-bolted thunder?
In the most terrible and nimble stroke
Of quick, cross lightning? to watch—poor perdu!—
With this thin helm? Mine enemy's dog,
Thought he had bit me, should have stood that night
Against my fire; and wast thou fain, poor father,
To hovel thee with swine, and rogues forlorn,
In short and musty straw? Alack, alack!

'Tis wonder that thy life and wits at once
Had not concluded all. He wakes!
How does my royal lord? How fares your majesty?
      O, look upon me, sir,
And hold your hands in benediction o'er me [.]

Antony and Cleopatra
CLEOPATRA—ACT I, SCENE 3

AGE: Any age (Mature)   INTENT: Serious

Shakespeare was writing about co-dependency long before it
became fashionable jargon to toss about. Historically, one
of the most infamous co-dependent couples was Antony and
Cleopatra. They lost friends, reputations, and empires because
they could not keep apart. Of the late tragedies, *Antony and
Cleopatra* is the only one that is a love tragedy—or rather the
downfall of the principals is brought about by unbridled
passion for each other. Cleopatra bedazzled Antony's faculties,
bewitched his fancy, and bewildered his judgment. She was for
Antony the kind of enchantment from which his rational senses
wanted to rebel but could not escape. At turns Cleopatra used
all of her wit and wiles, allurements, and vivacious imagination
to play the sorceress to hold Antony—object of her passion.
Against such caprices and voluptuousness, Antony didn't stand
a chance, for he was the most pathetic of victims: the brave soldier who collaborated willingly with his enemy to bring about
his own defeat.

But for all of her accomplishments, fascinations, and graces,
Cleopatra was, as all co-dependents seem to be, insecure in her
control. She always lived in fear of losing Antony unless he
was within eye-sight and hand's reach. Business and the ne-
cessity of ruling one-third of a great part of the known world
has called Antony back to Rome. Cleopatra, who is no stranger
to the calls of power nor to Rome, is desperate for Antony not
to leave Alexandria—and all the reasons are personal, nothing

of State. If passion and pleading will not stay him, perhaps petulance and childish conniving will.

CLEOPATRA

Pray you, stand farther from me.
I know, by that same eye, there's some good news.
What says the married woman? You may go:
Would she had never given you leave to come!
Let her not say 'tis I that keep you here:
I have no power upon you; hers you are
                    O, never was there queen
So mightily betray'd! yet at the first
I saw the treasons planted.
Why should I think that you can be mine and true,
Though you in swearing shake the throned gods,
Who have been false to Fulvia? Riotous madness,
To be entangled with those mouth-made vows,
Which break themselves in swearing!
Nay, pray you, seek no colour for your going,
But bid farewell, and go: when you sued staying,
Then was the time for words: no going then;
Eternity was in our lips and eyes,
Bliss in our brows' bent; none our parts so poor,
But was a race of heaven: they are so still,
Or thou, the greatest soldier of the world,
Art turned the greatest liar.
I would I had thy inches; thou shouldst know
There were a heart in Egypt.

Antony and Cleopatra
CLEOPATRA—ACT I, SCENE 5

AGE: Any age (Mature)   INTENT: Humorous

Antony has been away from Alexandria for some time, but Cleopatra's thoughts are never far from him. Strangely enough, with all of her insecurity, at this point she seems confident of her control over her lover, and she doesn't seem too concerned with what Antony may be doing with whom. And to Antony's credit in their relationship, Cleopatra finds life less than scintillating with him gone. Here, she is in her palace at Alexandria, surrounded by her attendants, Charmian, Iras, and the eunuch, Mardian, fully engrossed in her favorite occupation, more time consuming than even that of a ruling monarch: speculating about Antony.

CLEOPATRA

O Charmian,
Where think'st thou he is now? Stands he, or sits he?
Or does he walk? or is he on his horse?
O happy horse, to bear the weight of Antony!
Do bravely, horse! for wot'st thou whom thou movest?
The demi-Atlas of this earth, the arm
And burgonet of men. He's speaking now,
Or murmuring 'Where's my serpent of old Nile?'
For so he calls me: now I feed myself
With most delicious poison. Think on me,
That am with Phoebus' amorous pinches black,
And wrinkled deep in time? Broad-fronted Caesar,
When thou wast here above the ground, I was
A morsel for a monarch: and great Pompey
Would stand and make his eyes grow in my brow;
There would he anchor his aspect and die
With looking on is life.

PART IV: THE ROMANCES
AND THE
"PROBLEM PLAYS"

Troilus and Cressida
CRESSIDA—ACT III, SCENE 2

AGE: Young   INTENT: Serious

The legend of Troilus and Cressida was well known to the Elizabethans, due in part to one of the sources of the play, Chaucer's poem *Troilus and Criseyde*. Elizabethans also had an affinity for the Trojans because one branch of their history held that England was also founded by a group of refugee Trojans escaping from the nasty Greeks after the fall of Troy. But in all of these stories and legends, Cressida does not come out with shimmering character references. Cressida has passed into synonymous meaning of fickleness and falsehood.

Cressida is the daughter of Calchas, a Trojan priest, who has deserted Troy and joined with the Greeks, while his daughter has remained with the city. Troilus is one of the many sons of that over-productive king, Priam. Troilus falls in love with Cressida, passionately and obsessively and honestly. Cressida, unfortunately, is one of these women who, if she is "not near the man she loves, loves the man she is near." Cressida is beautiful and witty; she is good company; she is also passionate and coquettish, so, therefore, she is ardent and inconstant rather that affectionate and steady. She is also a pawn of the war. She is exchanged, at the request of her father, for the Trojan commander Antenor, and she is sent to the Greek camp. Once there, she forgets Troilus and takes up with a Greek prince, Diomedes.

After the longest time of playing go-between and matchmaker, Cressida's uncle, Pandarus, has finally arranged a successful, private assignation between the two young people in the orchard of his home. While Pandarus has been ever busy taking impressions and messages back and forth between them, this is the first extended, secluded meeting between Troilus and Cressida. Both of them know exactly what they want from this encounter and how they want it to end, even though Pandarus hovers about, solicitous and unsure.

CRESSIDA

Well, uncle, what folly I commit, I dedicate to you.
Boldness comes to me now, and brings me heart.
Prince Troilus, I have loved you night and day
For many weary months.
Hard to seem won: but I was won, my lord,
With the first glance that ever—pardon me—
If I confess much, you will play the tyrant.
I love you now; but not, till now, so much
But I might master it: in faith, I lie;
My thoughts were like unbridled children, grown
Too headstrong for their mother. See, we fools!
Why have I blabb'd? who shall be true to us,
When we are so unsecret to ourselves?
But, though I loved you well, I woo'd you not:
And yet, good faith, I wish'd myself a man,
Or that we women had men's privilege
Of speaking first. Sweet, bid me hold my tongue,
For in this rapture I shall surely speak
The thing I shall repent. See, see, your silence,
Cunning in dumbness, from my weakness draws
My very soul of counsel! stop my mouth.
My lord, I do beseech you, pardon me;
"Twas not my purpose, thus to beg and kiss:
I am ashamed. O heavens! what have I done?
For this time will I take leave, my lord.

All's Well that Ends Well
HELENA—ACT I, SCENE 1

AGE: Young   INTENT: Serious

Helena is the daughter of an accomplished physician, and she has learned his art. She is of the gentry, not the nobility, and she also has fallen in love with the young and callow Count Bertram. It is a love that is not returned. On the surface, Helena appears to be a straight-forward, innocent, and simple girl; but she possesses an indomitable inner spirit and inner strength. She seems always to be clear-headed about the solutions to the increasingly complicated dilemmas she encounters.

The first dilemma Helena faces is how to get Bertram to notice her, romantically, and then how to win him. Helena has just bid an empty farewell to Bertram, who has been summoned to the King's court, and she has just repelled the advances of Bertram's soldier companion, the braggadocio, Parolles. After these back-to-back incidents, Helena realizes that it is she, and she alone, that must gauge and govern the actions that will conclude her desired destiny.

HELENA

Our remedies oft on ourselves do lie,
Which we ascribe to heaven: the fated sky
Gives us free scope, only doth backward pull
Our slow designs when we ourselves are dull.
What power is it which mounts my love so high,
That makes me see, and cannot feed mine eye?
The mightiest space in fortune nature brings
To join like likes and kiss like native things.
Impossible be strange attempts to those
That weigh their pains in sense and do no suppose
What hath been cannot be: who ever strove

To show her merit, that did miss her love?
The king's disease—my project may deceive me,
But my intents are fix'd and will not leave me.

All's Well that Ends Well
COUNTESS—ACT III, SCENE 4

AGE: Mature   INTENT: Serious

Bernard Shaw once called the Countess of Rossillion the
best "old lady's part" Shakespeare ever wrote. Without a
doubt, the Countess is a wonderful part, but there is nothing
necessarily "old" about her. She is a widow and the mother of
the present adolescent count, Bertram, so she has acquired the
appellation Dowager Countess, but this does not mean she's
ready for a Bath chair and hot milk. But the Countess does require an actress of both experience and ability to portray her
striking qualities.

The Countess is affectionate, clear-sighted, and just. She
does not let love for her son blind her to his faults or to his er-
rors; nor does she allow her pride in her own rank and dignity
to shade he perception of the virtues and the abilities of those
lower born than she, especially the gentlewoman, Helena,
whom she has raised as a daughter; and she is the girl's
protectress. The Countess is, for her time, a true "democrat."

Count Bertram has been forced to marry Helena by orders of
the King of France. Bertram has done so with great hostility.
He has also sent his new wife to his mother at Rossillion while
he steals off to the wars in Italy. He writes to his wife a
devastating letter, renouncing his marriage and outlining
impossible conditions by which he would acknowledge it.
Helena, not to be deterred by such rejection, has followed, also
by stealth, Bertram to Florence. She has done this by night,
leaving a letter to inform the Countess of her actions. The
Countess is with her household steward, Rynaldo, who has read

the girl's letter to his Lady Countess a number of times. The
Countess is still shaken by Helena's words.

COUNTESS

Alas! and would you take the letter of her?
Might you not know she would do as she has done
By sending me a letter?
Ah, what sharp stings are in her mildest words!
Rynaldo, you did never lack advice so much
As letting her pass so; had I spoke with her,
I could have well diverted her intents,
Which thus she hath prevented. What angel shall
Bless this unworthy husband? He cannot thrive,
Unless her prayers, whom heaven delights to hear
And loves to grant, reprieve him from the wrath
Of greatest justice. Write, write, Rynaldo,
To this unworthy husband of his wife;
Let every word weigh heavy on her worth
That he does weigh too light; my greatest grief,
Though little he do feel it, set down sharply.
Dispatch the most convenient messenger.
When haply he shall hear that she is gone,
He will return; and hope I may that she,
Hearing so much, will speed her foot again,
Led hither by pure love. Which of them both
Is dearest to me I have no skill in sense
To make distinction. Provide this messenger.
My heart is heavy and mine age is weak;
Grief would have tears and sorrow bids me speak.
                    [Exit.]

Measure for Measure
ISABELLA—ACT II, SCENE 4

AGE: Any age (Young)   INTENT: Serious

Vincentio, duke of Vienna, has for a brief time turned the reins of government over to his deputy, Lord Angelo, assigning him all of his powers and duties, while the duke "retreats" for meditation. (Secretly, however, the duke remains in the city to see how his government and justice works in his realm.) Lord Angelo is a hard, unbending, and puritanical man. One of his first decrees is to condemn Claudio to death for sleeping with a woman he is unable to marry. Claudio begs his sister, Isabella, a novice in the Order of Ste. Clare, to intercede with Angelo on his behalf. She agrees, and from the first moment he sees her, lust enters Angelo's eyes, mind, heart, and loins. The only way the chaste and good Isabella may "redeem thy brother" is "by yielding up thy body" to Angelo.

Isabella has just endured an interview with Lord Angelo in which he has made the offer he didn't think she would refuse: her body for the life of her brother. But she did refuse, and repels Angelo's advances with a front of her own: if he does not give a pardon to Claudio, she will announce his perfidy to the world. But Angelo has a counter for every threat. Who would believe her, he asks. His "unsoil'd name, the austereness of [his] life" would work against her, and his rank in the State would out weigh her accusations. Angelo is so put out at Isabella's non-acquiescence to his demand he tells her that if she does not submit, not only will Claudio die, but Angelo will see that it is a death of "lingering sufferance"—and it will be her fault the way Claudio dies. Angelo has just left Isabella, giving her twenty-four hours to return with the expected answer to his demand. She is alone, except for her goodness and her God.

ISABELLA

To whom should I complain? Did I tell this,
Who would believe me? O perilous mouths,
That bear in them one and the self-same tongue,
Either of condemnation or approof;
Bidding the law make court'sy to their will;
Hooking both right and wrong to the appetite,
To follow as it draws! I'll to my brother:
Though he hath fall'n by prompture of the blood,
Yet hath he in him such a mind of honour,
That, had he twenty heads to tender down
On twenty bloody blocks, he'ld yield them up,
Before his sister should her body stoop
To such abhorr'd pollution.
Then, Isabel, live chaste, and brother, die:
More than our brother is our chastity.
I'll tell him yet of Angelo's request,
And fit his mind to death, for his soul's rest.

Pericles
MARINA—ACT V, SCENE 1

AGE: Young   INTENT: Serious

Pericles was an extremely popular and successful play in Shakespeare's theater, which is an interesting piece of information when one considers how unsatisfactory is the text of the play that has come down to us. *Pericles* is an "adventurous" play, not only in its chronicle of the hero's escapades and trials, but also in the manner in which Shakespeare wrote it. "Experimental" is the operative word.

All of the adventures in the play are painful ones. Marina has been born at sea, her mother thought to have died in childbirth, and the coffin containing the body tossed overboard into the sea. Marina is raised at Pericles' behest by foster parents, the governor of Tarsus and his wife, Dionyza. Marina outshines her foster sister, so Dionyza plots to have Marina murdered. But Marina is "rescued" from the murder by pirates who sell her into a brothel in Mytilene. She manages to escape the brothel and "chances/Into an honest house," where her reputation as a superlative entertainer and a maid of virtue blossoms. Finally, she is reunited with her father through incredulous circumstances when she is called upon, aboard ship, to cure Pericles and induce the grieving Pericles to speak for the first time in over three months. Pericles has been committing slow suicide by silence and starvation and isolation driven by grief over the "deaths" of his wife and daughter.

This is the moment in which Marina reveals herself to her father, who, of course, does not recognize her. Marina is completely ingenuous and guileless, telling her story with all simplicity of truth. (She has, by the way, just finished singing a lyrical ditty that has captured Pericles' attention and moved him to speak for the first time—to anyone—in three months. Marina embodies grace and enchantment, if nothing else.)

MARINA

I am a maid,
My lord, that ne'er before invited eyes,
But have been gazed on like a comet: she speaks,
My lord, that, may be, hath endured a grief
Might equal yours, if both were justly weigh'd.
Through wayward fortune did malign my state,
My derivation was from ancestors
Who stood equivalent with mighty kings:
But time hath rooted out my parentage,
And to the world and awkward casualties
Bound me in servitude. [*Aside*] I will desist:
But there is something glows upon my cheek,
And whispers in mine ear "Go not till he speak.'
I said, my lord, if you did know my parentage,

You would not do me violence.
If I should tell my history, it would seem
Like lies disdain'd in the reporting.
My name is Marina.
The name
Was given me by one that had some power,
My father, and a king. Call'd Marina
For I was born at sea.
My mother was the daughter of a king;
Who died the minute I was born,
As my good nurse Lychorida hath oft
Deliver'd weeping.
The king my father did in Tarsus leave me;
Till cruel Cleon, with his wicked wife,
Did seek to murder me: and having woo'd
A villain to attempt it, who having drawn to do't,
A crew of pirates came and rescued me;
Brought me to Mytilene. But, good sir,
Whither will you have me? Why do you weep?
It may be,
You think me an imposter: no good faith;
I am the daughter of King Pericles,
If good King Pericles be.

The Tempest
MIRANDA—ACT I, SCENE 2

AGE: Young   INTENT: Serious

Miranda has experienced more than once in her isolated life the fury of her angry, magician father, Prospero. She has seen the results of his temper when his wrath and fury have found expression in his "so potent art." Miranda's knowledge of men and of other worlds is, of course, lacking, but she is not lacking in the natural milk of human kindness and the concern for the welfare of others when witnessing their torments from a

safe distance. From somewhere on the island, Miranda has seen
the "tempest" roar up from the offshore and clutch at the vessel
which contained her (unknown) uncle, the King of Naples,
Ferdinand, and all the rest. She was terrified at the power of the
storm, but she was also wise enough to realize, since the tempest storm did not disturb the enchanted isle that is her home,
that her father and his magic may have something to do with
it—if not totally responsible for it. Miranda is a girl of fifteen,
just beginning to enter into her womanhood, and just becoming
absorbed and concerned with life. And she is full of the worries
one has at that age, about the inequities of the world—and the
aches of idealism to do something about them.

MIRANDA

If by your art, my dearest father, you have
Put the wild waters in this roar, allay them.
The sky, it seems, would pour down stinking pitch,
But that the sea, mounting to the welkin's cheek,
Dashes the fire out. O, I have suffer'd
With those that I saw suffer: a brave vessel,
Who had, no doubt, some noble creature in her,
Dash'd all to pieces. O, the cry did knock
Against my heart. Poor souls, they perish'd.
Had I been any god of power, I would
Have sunk the sea within the earth or ere
It should the good ship so have swallow'd and
The fraughting souls within her.